BUILDING BLOCKS OF COMPUTER SCIENCE

CODING: LANGUAGES AND ORDER

Written by Echo Elise González

Illustrated by Graham Ross

www.worldbook.com

Co-published by agreement between Shi Tu Hui and World Book, Inc.

Shi Tu Hui
Room 1807, Block 1,
#3 West Dawang Road
Chaoyang District, Beijing 100025
P.R. China

World Book, Inc.
180 North LaSalle Street
Suite 900
Chicago, Illinois 60601
USA

© 2026. All rights reserved. This volume may not be reproduced in whole or in part in any form without prior written permission from the publisher.

WORLD BOOK and the GLOBE DEVICE are registered trademarks or trademarks of World Book, Inc.

Library of Congress Control Number: 2025938324

Building Blocks of Computer Science
ISBN: 978-0-7166-6706-3 (set, hard cover)

Coding: Languages and Order
ISBN: 978-0-7166-6707-0 (hard cover)

Also available as:
ISBN: 978-0-7166-6717-9 (soft cover)
ISBN: 978-0-7166-6727-8 (e-book)

WORLD BOOK STAFF

Editorial

Vice President
Tom Evans

Senior Manager, New Content
Jeff De La Rosa

Manager, New Product Development
Nicholas Kilzer

Associate Manager, New Content
William D. Adams

Content Creator
Elizabeth Huyck

Proofreader
Nathalie Strassheim

Graphics and Design

Senior Visual Communications Designer
Melanie Bender

Acknowledgments

Writer: Echo Elise González
Illustrator: Graham Ross/The Bright Agency
Series reviewed by George K. Thiruvathukal (Loyola University Chicago); Peter Jang (Actualize Coding Bootcamp)

TABLE OF CONTENTS

What Is Coding Language? 4
Machine Language 8
High-Level Languages 12
So, How Do They Work? 14
Which Language Should You Learn? 18
Order! 20
Control Flow 22
Sequencing 26
Selection 28
Iteration 30
Data Sorting 32
Data-Sorting Algorithms 36
Words to Know and Index 40

There is a glossary on page 40. Terms defined in the glossary are in type **that looks like this** on their first appearance.

There are many kinds of coding languages. Different languages can be used on different types of machines and for different purposes.

Coding languages can be organized into two categories: **high-level languages** and **low-level languages**.

Coders use high-level languages to write computer programs.

```
#Leap Year Check
if year % 4=0 and
year % 100!=0:
print (year, "is a
leap year")
```

Those programs are then converted into low-level languages—such as **assembly language** and machine language—for the computer to read.

```
10101010111001010101010001
00101010001010010101010001
10110110001010110101001010
11001010100101010101000010
10101001010101000101010101
```

Assembly language is a language designed for one specific kind of **processor**, an information-processing **computer chip** that controls a computer system.

```
1010 10101010100101010100
0010100110101010001101
```

Programmers usually write code in high-level languages because low-level languages are difficult for humans to work with.

```
10100101011010
10100010101010
00010011010100
10110101000110
```

MACHINE LANGUAGE

Like humans, computers need their instructions given in a language they can understand.

Tasky the Robot, like all computers, understands machine language.

Instead of letters and words, machine language is made up of **bits.**

A bit is the tiniest piece of **data** a computer can store.

It's just a little bit of information... the littlest bit!

HIGH-LEVEL LANGUAGES

"Low-level languages can be very specific to one particular type of machine or even a single machine."

"But high-level languages can be used on a variety of machines."

"So, a programmer can use a high-level language to write a program that works on multiple different machines, not just one."

To write a computer program in a low-level language, a programmer would have to write huge amounts of complex code to control the **hardware** of that specific machine.

The programmer would have to write a separate program for each individual computer!

With a high-level language, the programmer only has to write the program once.

Coding in high-level languages is therefore much more efficient than using low-level languages.

TAP TAP

We use syntax when we're speaking or writing to make sure our sentences are understandable to others.

Similarly, programmers use syntax rules to define the grammar and order of a coding language.

Syntax helps them to create lines of code that the computer can understand.

Writing a line of code that doesn't use proper syntax results in a syntax error.

In human language, forgetting a comma or adding an extra period could be a bit confusing, but it probably wouldn't stop the reader from understanding the meaning of the sentence.

But making a punctuation mistake in a computer program usually means that the computer won't be able to understand the instructions at all!

Coding languages are designed to create instructions that are very clear.

Many programmers start off learning a simple language that is easy to get the hang of.

Many want to learn a general-purpose language that can be used for as many applications as possible.

Others prefer to learn a language that is made for a specific purpose, such as developing **artificial intelligence** or working with **databases.**

Whichever language you end up learning, just remember: It's okay to take it slow.

If you're patient, you can learn as many as you like!

Maybe someday, you'll even create your own coding language!

SEQUENCING

In a sequenced control flow, the computer program runs in the order the code is entered.

The computer simply reads a sequenced program from top to bottom, one line at a time.

Sequenced control flows work well for many straightforward computer programs.

Let's use sequencing to put this burger together.

A sequenced control flow is perfect for this task, because we only need to add the ingredients one at a time until the sandwich is complete.

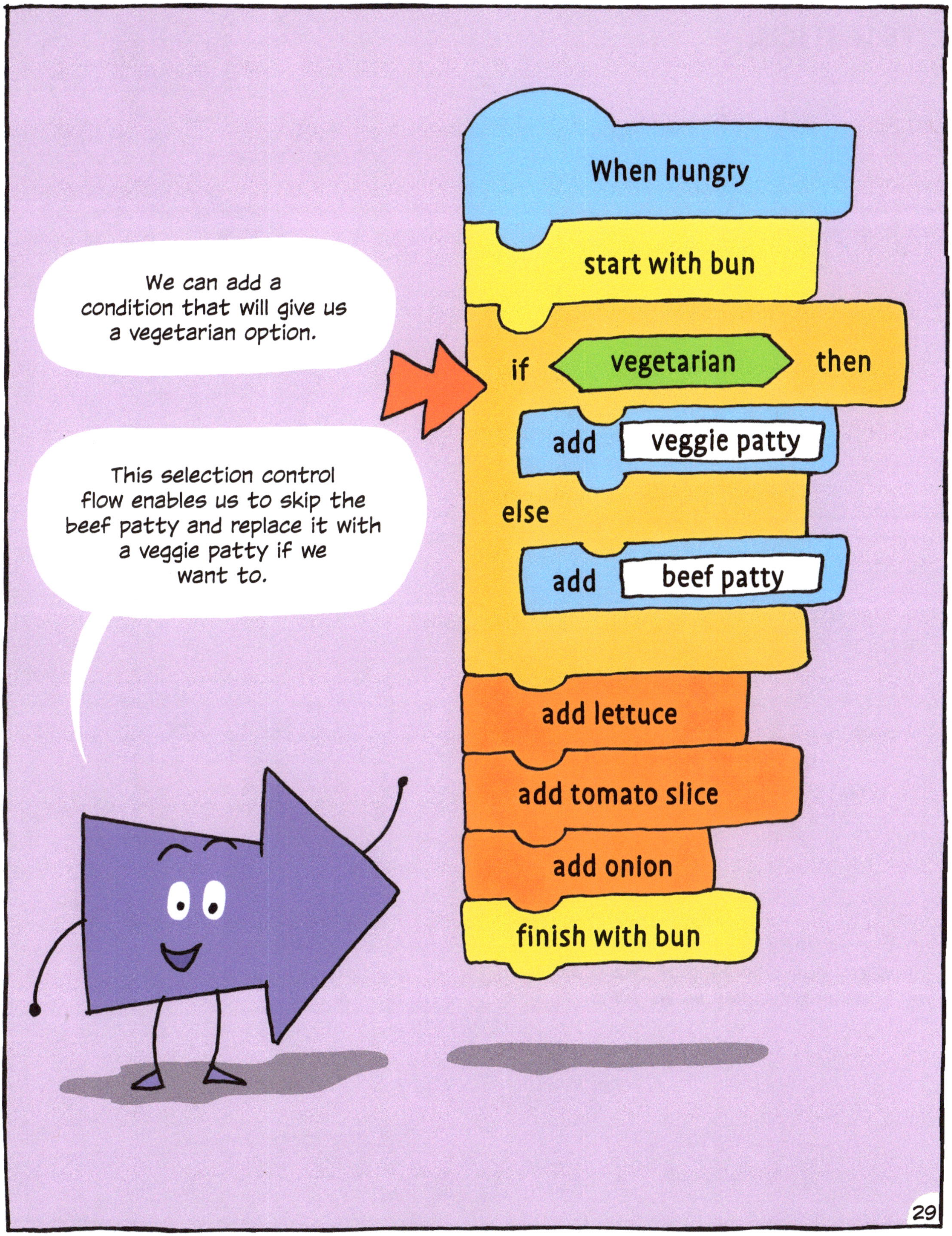

We can add a condition that will give us a vegetarian option.

This selection control flow enables us to skip the beef patty and replace it with a veggie patty if we want to.

When hungry

start with bun

if vegetarian then

add veggie patty

else

add beef patty

add lettuce

add tomato slice

add onion

finish with bun

ITERATION

I'm hungry.

Let's write a program to eat the hamburger we built!

We can use an iteration control flow to make this program.

Here are code blocks for taking a bite, chewing, and swallowing.

These steps must be done multiple times, over and over again, until the hamburger is finished.

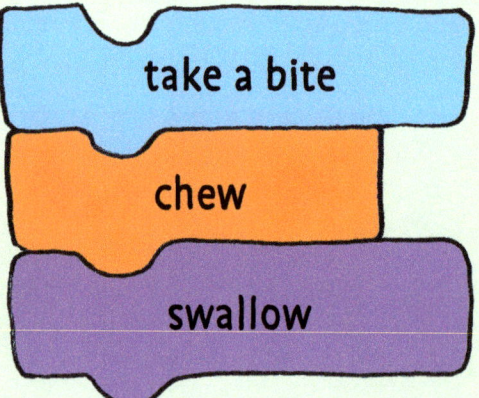

So, let's use iteration to carry out this part of the code as many times as we want.

I'll add a **loop** to repeat this part.

Now, I don't have to add these same blocks over and over again!

REPEAT
take a bite
chew
swallow

Looks like the sandwich-eating program is ready to run!

NOM! NOM! NOM!

Whether we are sorting the data that makes up a program...

Or organizing the program itself in a way that produces the result we want...

We always want to go with the flow.

It's all about order!

39

WORDS TO KNOW

algorithm a set of step-by-step instructions used to write computer programs.

artificial intelligence a kind of computer program that uses data and logic to solve complex problems.

assembler a program that translates each command in a low-level **assembly language** into a command in machine language.

binary digit a 0 or 1. These are the two digits that make up machine language.

bit the smallest piece of data a computer can store. A bit is represented by a 0 or a 1.

byte a group of eight bits. A **gigabyte** is 1 billion bytes.

coding language or **programming language** a set of symbols and rules that programmers use to write computer programs.

compiler a program that translates a high-level language into an assembly language.

computer chip a small chip of silicon holding tiny electronic circuits that perform logic functions.

condition a statement that can be true or false. A program may tell a computer to run a piece of code if a certain condition is true.

control flow the order in which a computer follows the steps of a computer program.

data information that a computer processes or stores. A **database** is an organized collection of data.

divide-and-conquer a data-sorting strategy in which data is divided, then recombined in a particular order.

hardware the physical parts that make up computers and other electronics.

high-level language a programming language that uses symbols and words that human programmers can more easily understand.

iteration a control flow in which certain lines of code are repeated.

loop a piece of code that causes part of a program to run over and over again.

low-level language the code used to communicate programs to a computer's hardware. High-level languages are translated into low-level languages for the computer to understand.

machine language the code used to communicate programs to a computer's hardware. Machine language is made up of binary digits.

processor a kind of computer chip that performs calculations for the computer.

selection a control flow in which certain lines of code are skipped over unless certain conditions are true.

sequencing a control flow in which the computer program follows the steps of code in order.

spreadsheet a document in which data is arranged in rows and columns.

syntax the rules that make up the "grammar" of a programming language. A **syntax error** is an error caused by improper syntax in the code.

variable a value, or piece of information, that can change.

INDEX

algorithms, 21, 34-37
artificial intelligence (AI), 19
assembler, 7
assembly language, 6

binary digits, 4, 7
bits, 8-11
byte, 11

circuits, 9
coding languages, 4-7
  high-level, 6-7, 12-13
  kinds of, 6-13, 18-19
  learning, 18-19
  low-level, 6-7, 12-13
  translating, 4-7
compiler, 7
computer programmers, 5, 6, 12-13, 15, 16, 19, 21, 22, 24, 25, 34, 36, 38
conditions, 16, 22, 24, 25, 28, 29

control flow, 20-25; kinds of 24-31; sorting, 32-35

data, 8, 34-37, 39
data sorting, 21, 32-37, 39
databases, 19
divide-and-conquer method, 37

gigabyte, 11

iteration, 24-25, 30-31

loops, 16, 22, 24, 31

machine language, 4, 6-13

processor, 9
programming languages. See coding languages
punctuation, 16-17

selection, 24-25, 28-29
sequencing, 24-27
spreadsheet, 36
syntax, 14-17
syntax error, 15

text-based languages, 16

variables, 16
video games, 11, 36

websites, 36

www.ingramcontent.com/pod-product-compliance
Lightning Source LLC
Chambersburg PA
CBHW061256170426
43191CB00041B/2433